Blockchain Applied: Solving legacy system problems across multiple industries with distributed ledger technology

Solutions for Healthcare, Supply Chain, Insurance, Banking, Financial Markets & Trading Systems, Media & Entertainment, Critical Infrastructure Security and Real Estate

Blockchain in Healthcare & Pharmaceuticals Industry

According to the World Health Organization (WHO), 1 in 10 medical products in developing countries is falsified or substandard. The impact on personal and public health is estimated in the region upwards of **$200 billion annually**. According to a Pfizer-sponsored survey, Western Europeans spend an estimated 10.5 billion euros ($14.3 billion) a year on illicitly sourced medicines. According to Boyd **Insurance**, Medicare fraud in the U.S. alone costs about $68 billion a year.

In developing countries each year, more than 250,000 children with malaria and pneumonia, common illnesses do not survive after being treated with fake and substandard drugs. Around 30% of drugs that are sold in developing and third-world countries are considered to be counterfeits. Inspection and approval mechanisms are mostly inefficient or even non-existent in some cases. On the technical side, expensive analytic equipment generally isn't available, while simple, accurate, and inexpensive testing systems for use in the field, at pharmacies, and at points of care remain out of reach for most communities.

Blockchain opens up the possibility of truly placing the patient at the centre of the healthcare ecosystem. A blockchain system could ensure a chain-of-custody log, tracking each step of the supply chain. The technology has the potential to also transform the industry through increased the security, privacy, and interoperability of health data. New models for health information exchanges are being build which make electronic medical records more efficient, disintermediated, and secure. Blockchain is seen as a powerful tool that can also help cut costs, carry out effective relief efforts, improve medical record keeping or access, and much more.

By 2020, global annual health spending is expected to reach over $8.734 trillion. According to a **report by BIS research**, by 2025, the healthcare industry can save up to $100 billion per year in data breach-related costs, IT costs, operations costs, support function and personnel costs, counterfeit-related frauds and insurance frauds if they incorporate the blockchain technology.

The report also states that the use of "*a global blockchain in the healthcare market is expected grow at a CAGR of 63.85% from 2018 to 2025, to reach a value of $5.61 billion by 2025. The use of blockchain for healthcare data exchange will contribute the largest market share throughout the forecast period, reaching a value of $1.89 billion by 2025, owing to the use of blockchain to solve the most widespread problem in* *healthcare information systems related to interoperability and non-standardization that has created data silos in the industry."*

The promise of blockchain has widespread implications for stakeholders in the health care ecosystem. Taking advantage of the benefits of this technology can connect fragmented systems to generate insights and to better assess the value of care through blockchain powered health information exchanges which unlock the true value of interoperability. With blockchain-based systems, a reduction of systematic friction and costs can be achieved and in the long run, blockchain networks for electronic medical records are expected to improve efficiencies and support better health outcomes for patients.

Numerous researchers forecast that over half of healthcare applications will have adopted blockchain for commercial deployment by 2025 but currently, healthcare institutions face challenges including an inability to securely share data across platforms. However, improved data collaboration between providers could result in a higher probability of accurate diagnoses, higher likelihood of effective treatments, and an overall increased ability of healthcare systems to deliver cost-effective care. The implementation of blockchain technology could enable parties in the healthcare value chain to share access to their networks without compromising data security and integrity. Blockchain technology creates unique opportunities to reduce complexity, enable trustless collaboration, and create secure and immutable information.

Some players in the global blockchain in healthcare market include IBM Corporation, Accenture, Microsoft, Capgemini, and Deloitte Touche Tohmatsu Limited.
Startup **Gem** launched the Gem Health Network using Ethereum blockchain-enabled technology to create a secure, universal data-sharing infrastructure for the space. **Tierion** is another blockchain startup that has built a platform for data storage and verification in healthcare; both Gem and Tierion recently partnered with Philips Healthcare in the **Philips Blockchain Lab**. Another startup, **Hu-manity**, partnered with IBM on an electronic ledger that is trying to give patients more control over their data.

MedRec is a company that seeks to save the digital family history of medical records on an immutable blockchain database. MediLedger is reported to be using blockchain to strengthen the track-and-trace capabilities for prescription medicine. ConnectingCare is a platform for providers from different clinical organizations coming together to access the same data for shared patients on the blockchain. Robomed Network is a blockchain based medical network aimed at connecting patients and healthcare service providers using **smart contracts**.

Transforming the Supply Chain Landscape with Blockchain

It is estimated that the supply chain industry represents over $50 trillion in annual GDP globally. In a 2017 report by Statista, the global blockchain technology market is predicted to reach 339.5 million U.S. dollars in size and is forecast to grow to US$2.3 billion by 2021.

The supply chain management software industry was worth US$12.2 billion in 2017 according to **Statista** and the market is predicted to exceed $19 billion in total software revenue by 2021, according to global research and advisory firm **Gartner**.

Current supply chain solutions are expensive. It is also a fact that companies with global supply chains could be standing on a cost base of which 90% is attributable to supply chain expenditure. According to a survey by **Deloitte** from 2014, 79% of companies with high-performing supply chains achieve revenue growth greater than the average within their industries. Conversely, just 8% of businesses with less capable supply chains report above-average growth.

According to the **Logistics Bureau**, a 2014 survey conducted by PwC revealed that businesses with optimal supply chains have 15% lower supply chain costs, less than 50% of the inventory holdings and cash-to-cash cycles that are at least three times faster than those not focused on supply chain optimization. In another study conducted by Aberdeen group in 2013, top-performing companies that implemented supplier performance management initiatives had achieved average cost savings of around 12%.

Transforming supply chain with blockchain

Blockchain has tremendous potential for transforming supply chains and disrupting the way we produce, market, purchase and consume goods. Managing supply chains involves managing flows between the source of the raw materials all the way to the end customer. According to the _Fidelity Global Institutional Investor Survey: The Future of Investment Management_, 73% percent of institutional investors agree that a new asset class will emerge due to advances in technologies such as blockchain.

Traditional supply chain management systems make it difficult for customers or buyers to accurately determine the value of products due to the lack of transparency. Even when there is suspected illegal or unethical practices, the current state of supply chains makes it extremely cumbersome to investigate and get to the root of the problems. All this makes centralised supply chains very inefficient, but the elasticity of blockchain offers a much-needed solution because it can be modelled in different ways to fit different processes, network node architectures, and participants.

The built-in chain of command offered by blockchain ultimately means the technology can increase efficiency and transparency of supply chains and positively impact everything from warehousing to delivery to payment.

Blockchain-based supply chain management systems offer a decentralised approach to data management and sharing by minimising the involvement of intermediaries such as bankers, insurers, and brokers. In addition, these new supply chain management solutions help to establish better proof of quality, provenance, payment, and performance to minimise counterfeiting and fraud.

Furthermore, blockchain technology enables time-stamping, tracking, automation of transactions, and even real-time verification and auditing. Through blockchains, companies gain a real-time digital ledger of transactions and movements for all participants in their supply chain network.

According to EY Global Innovation Blockchain Leader, Paul Brody, "*It's important to clarify that the blockchain isn't merely a prerequisite piece of software to buy. It's actually the opposite — a solution to current fragmented supply chain infrastructure.*"

Blockchain enables triple entry accounting. Instead of simply having debits and credits, there is another entry on the blockchain which makes real-time auditing possible. When it comes to the US$64 trillion supply chain industry, the impact that blockchain technology will potentially have on this enormous industry is enormous.

Some of the areas of supply chain management which can benefit from blockchain include:

- Fraud prevention due to the immutable records on the blockchain
- Increased transparency and better authentication protocols
- Overall improved efficiency and better business relations which positively impact the business involvement.
- Recording quantity and type of goods or commodities being shipped
- Maintaining order tracking and logistics information
- Payment automation via smart contracts
- Process management to improve client service delivery

Benefits

At the rudimentary level, the core logic of blockchains means that a single piece of inventory cannot exist in the same place twice and that every movement of a product or asset is visible to all supply chain participants in near real-time with full traceability back to the point of origin.

Provenance in supply chain is vital to prove the authenticity of a shipment or the origin of a product. Not only is this important to end-consumers but also to all participants in a specific supply chain. Blockchain applications make use of this by tracing back along the information flow to certain verified data points. Tracing a product back to its original manufacturer to assess its genuineness can be crucial especially where a distributor or retailer is not able to trust the wholesaler.

Using blockchain also means that businesses can negotiate procurement deals based on total ecosystem volumes, not just what they purchase from an individual supplier. Ultimately, blockchain-based solutions enable:

- Calculations of exact volume discounts based on total purchasing
- Proof of transaction data accuracy
- Preservation of privacy of each company's individual volumes and protection of their competitive advantage
- Better visibility into procurement
- Increased trust among all participants in supply chain networks
- Accurate and reliable data for analytics

- Better procurement which means more visibility and more savings
- Improved data and analytics and consequently better outcomes

Identifying areas where blockchain could enhance supply chain processes, but also where distributed databases would be better than a blockchain database, will be key to achieving maximum efficiency. To give maximum viability to any blockchain-based supply chain management company's value proposition, understanding that the processing power of decentralised blockchain databases may not be as efficient as a centralised system due to performance speeds is important, because only then can an innovative and new approach be introduced.

Blockchain technology has already begun to impact several aspects of businesses because it provides a complete chain of custody for items that are stored on these distributed ledgers from their origin to point of sale. In addition, users are able to trust the data on the chain due to its immutability. Blockchain's tracking capabilities also enable full audit trails, which give companies confidence in the authenticity and quality of goods. The distributed nature of the decentralised platforms allows for better oversight and control of products, while real-time tracking via smart contracts offers supply chain participants the flexibility to make faster decisions and keep more accurate track of inventory levels, ultimately reducing working capital inactivity.

One of the most universally applicable aspects of blockchain is that it enables more secure, transparent monitoring of transactions. Supply chains are basically a series of transaction nodes that link to move products from point A to the point-of-sale or final deployment. With blockchain, as products change hands across a supply chain from manufacture to sale, the transactions can be documented in a permanent decentralised record — reducing time delays, added costs, and human errors.

Use Case Example:
The supply chain of an automotive business, for example, can be a particularly impressive use case for a distributed ledger solution. The automotive industry is highly regulated and has cross-country regulators, multiple network participants and a growing data storage challenge in this new world of big data. A blockchain-based solution can help keep track of the exact record of each and every part that went into an automobile or parts that were replaced, its manufacturing and transportation history, and sales and resale history, all while providing regulators the information they need to ensure compliance. Smart contracts on blockchains can even facilitate the transfer of ownership.

Many supply chains have a dominant entity. For example, in an automotive supply chain, the manufacturer is certainly the most powerful player, and the rest of suppliers and distributors are often highly dependent on it — both for goods and the rate of technological advancement within the industry. In such a case, the manufacturer can enforce a blockchain-based supply chain implementation that everyone else in the chain will have to adopt. **EY** predicts a blockchain across the entire automotive marketplace.

Solving the problems of counterfeit parts by determining provenance can help tackle the problem of counterfeit parts within automotive supply chains. By deploying blockchain technology for supply chain logistics, original equipment manufacturers can finally obtain a solution to a serious challenge they have been facing for decades. The capability of tracing a part through every step of the supply chain can ensure the part shipped is the part that will eventually arrive at the destination. As **IBM** highlights, this isn't just relevant to the auto industry; it can apply to any industry that relies on parts. Ultimately, blockchain is considered to offer enormous potential for improving processes and enhancing business models in logistics and supply chain management overall.

Developments

Several blockchain startups are innovating into this sector: **Provenance**, for one, is building a traceability system for materials and products, enabling businesses to engage consumers at the point of sale with information gathered collaboratively from suppliers all along the supply chain (and thus substantiate product claims with trustworthy, real-time data).

Others include **Hijro** (formerly Fluent), which offers an alternative platform for lending into global supply chains, and **Skuchain**, which builds blockchain-based products for the business-to-business trade and supply chain finance market.

Ocean cargo giant A.P. Moller-Maersk and technology powerhouse IBM announced plans for a joint venture aimed at "providing a jointly developed global trade digitization platform that is built on open standards and designed for use by the entire global shipping ecosystem." They are hoping by utilizing blockchain they can address the need to provide more transparency and simplicity in the movement of goods across borders and trading zones. Walmart and Sam's Club joined IBM's Food Trust network, which uses a blockchain distributed ledger.

The government of Rwanda is working with UK-based startup **Circulor** with the goal of tracing and removing sources of funding for conflict materials. In June 2017, The Federal Maritime Commission issued a **press release** about hosting a

Brown Bag presentation on blockchain technology, including its applications, for use in government and shipping.

The One Belt One Road project linking Hong Kong and Rotterdam, is already using the blockchain for trade finance where buyers, sellers, various shippers, escrow agents, tax authorities and other players have access to a shared network database in real-time.

DHL released a trend report that noted that "global supply chains are notoriously complex, with a diverse set of stakeholders, varying interests, and many third-party intermediaries — challenges that blockchain is well suited to address." The report includes initial findings on a working prototype developed by DHL and Accenture, which tracks pharmaceuticals from the point of origin to the consumer, preventing tampering and errors.

Conclusion

Blockchains increasingly become an attractive option for supply chain management where the supply chain is owned or participated in by multiple parties, none of which in most instances wish to give complete control of record keeping to another party. In such cases, blockchains offer a better solution for maintaining shared databases. According to **Frost & Sullivan**, the penetration rate of blockchain technology in functional areas such as retailing and leasing, supply chain logistics, and smart manufacturing will hit 37.2 percent by 2025.

Making a blockchain-powered insurance industry reality

Insurance involves a risk transfer mechanism that entails a company taking a potential risk from a customer in form of a loss or damage caused by events beyond the control of the customer and in return the customer pays a fee called premium. These premiums are typically then reinvested which subsequently generates better revenue return for the insurance company.

The insurance industry has been a key component of the global economy based on the amount of premiums it generates, the scale of its investment and the essential social and economic role it plays in covering personal and business risk. However, currently, there are over 400 million people globally with no insurance cover according to the World Health Organisation.

Current state of the market

To understand how blockchain applications work to improve the insurance industry, it's important to understand the main actors that create, distribute, and hold policies. Insurance is protection against financial loss. It is a way to manage risk through a third-party and because of this blockchain can help insurers deliver on streamlined subrogation, a more transparent claims process, using shared loss histories to obtain data-driven insights on prospective customers for more sophisticated pricing, and supporting more efficient payments between insurers and third parties, especially during the claims process.

The future for blockchain in the insurance industry is still in the development stage and looking to scale and improve the current value chain and business model. With possibilities of lowering operational cost and automating redundant processes, it's the fastest advanced technology set to be widely used in the coming years as reflected in the high growth rate topping 110%. By 2020, Accenture strategy estimates that the use of modern technology could bring about a more disruptive model and create a digital platform for about 20% of the Property and Casualty Insurance market.

The insurance industry is under threat from a constant shift towards risk prevention as against risk cover, more availability of data and the continued investment in Insurtech startups. Business automation is expected to reduce the cost of claims by over 30% which means that insurance businesses are looking for ways to retain customers and optimise profit.

New models utilising blockchain are expected to enable growth, increase effectiveness, and reduce cost by automating key processes. The potential advantage of this technology would be increased transparency and accountability and reduced transaction costs. Many believe blockchain will make an impact in major areas of the insurance value chain including product development and delivery, underwriting process, payments, claims process and asset management with the ability to remove intermediaries from the value chain and give greater control to the customer in areas like ownership and management of their personal data and identity management.

A survey of about 526 insurance professionals carried out by Cognizant shows that the percentage of insurance professionals who believe that blockchain implementation would mean faster claim settlement (43%), reduce fraud (40%), improve record keeping (40%), streamline processes (38%) and provide greater transparency (38%).

Some insurance companies that are already exploring ways to exploit this technology include Aegon, Allianz, Munich Re, and Swiss Re who have already set up a combined pilot project known as B3i to explore blockchain. More collaboration is needed among insurance and reinsurance companies to allow for the development of blockchain enabled products and adoption. Some industry insiders argue that public blockchains, where all parties have access to every transaction on the ledger, are not feasible for the insurance industry due to privacy and security concerns and that private, permissioned blockchains will be more favoured. The issue of regulation to protect consumers from abuse and insurance companies from taking on too much risk are also a concern. Thus, legal and regulatory frameworks for insurance need to evolve and provide clear guidance for blockchain technology to see wide adoption.

Advantages of Decentralizing the Insurance Industry

Decentralising the insurance industry will assist with streamlining underwriting, claims, payment, and the reinsurance processes. With fewer players involved in all transactions and processes from start to finish, processes will be made more efficient and faster. Another huge benefit is the enabling of automated payments via smart contracts. Security is another main benefit of using blockchain for insurance. The industry continues to see a growing number of uninsured persons and valuables with fraudulent insurance cover.

In the UK, most insurance company have attributed the high cost of car insurance to the rising cost of claims inclusive of fraudulent claims thereby increasing the cost inclusive for honest motorist. In Nigeria, reports by the Nigerian Insurance Association says that over 12 million Nigerian motorists carry fake insurance papers and avoid buying insurance out of the estimated 180 million people despite the benefits from motor insurance cover. In South Africa, an estimated 35% of 4 wheelers and 70% of 2 wheelers drivers are uninsured due to the huge cost of premium and lack of transparency in the insurance process. Fraudulent claims payment cost the insurance sector about $80 billion a year across all lines of insurance which is roughly about 20% of the total claims payment annually.

Blockchain enabled processes and applications are expected to solve these challenges, reducing cost and building trust. An IBM Research in Australia demonstrates using a prototype, how the implementation of a pay-as-you-go car insurance application on blockchain would ensure that all the data pertaining to the customer's actual trip and usage premium payment made are transparently recorded so that all parties involved in the insurance contract including the driver, the insurance company, and the financial institution were applicable are confident that the data is tamper-proof and traceable.

Blockchain provides quality security through decentralisation. Instead of storing all data on central server or having a single entity control all information, insurance can operate on a peer-to-peer distributed network that provides advanced protection. It not only helps insurance companies avoid getting hacked or suffering through a costly server crash, it gives customers peace of mind that their information cannot be so easily bought or sold. Blockchain also has excellent potential for identity verification and document authentication to help prevent fraud. Peer-to-peer networks can also help to notarise documents and guarantee identity without the help of a third-party.

As things become error-free, trustless, and more efficient, the price of insurance premiums is likely to drop. Blockchain is projected to be able to reduce fraud by 15%-25%. Additionally, it will work to reduce all of the expenses that are incurred due to insurance fraud which could save the industry over US$10 billion. It is hoped that those savings will trickle down from insurance companies to the average insurance customer.

Since blockchain increases transparency, data becomes immutable and reliable. Data stores will also be accessible in a more secure way, opening the doors for real-time statistics and analyses to improve operations and further cut costs. The more reliable the data, the less room for mistakes which means insurance companies can better meet the ever-evolving needs of policyholders.

How Different Insurance Verticals Can Use Blockchain

Health Insurance

Blockchain can improve not only health insurance, but how health care providers operate. Health insurance helps to connect medical institutions with patients through advanced data analysis. It can also help those without coverage get covered faster, more comprehensively, and more affordably. All major healthcare players have something to gain from distributed ledger technology. Decentralised applications in healthcare can help match patients with providers in their area and automate the coverage process.

The need for patient confidentiality means that providers often don't have access to patients' full medical history, despite the $28B medical records market. Lack of data can lead to insurance claim denials, which costs hospitals $262B yearly and are cited as a significant factor in rising healthcare costs. Blockchain technology can encrypt patient information, facilitating the transfer of information while still protecting patient privacy. A single patient will typically see multiple doctors and specialists over the course of his life. Because there are so many different parties involved in healthcare, it's difficult to share and coordinate sensitive medical data between them.

Sharing data and cooperating is currently difficult in the healthcare industry for 2 primary reasons: first, the back-end infrastructure for medical records is hopelessly outdated. The market for providers of electronic medical records management software is expected to hit almost $40B by the year 2022. Different providers and insurers rely on different standards and formats for how they store patient data. Medical data often has to be reconciled by hand across hospitals, insurance companies, clinics, and pharmacies.

Second, rigid privacy laws lead to data silos within organisations. In the US, the Health Insurance Portability and Accountability Act (HIPAA) exists to help secure private patient data, but the negative side effect is that it makes it hard to coordinate patient care across various providers and insurers. The cost implications for this are dire. In the US, total spending on healthcare administration is more than 1.5x that of countries like Switzerland, Canada, Germany and France. The US spends 8% of its total healthcare expenditure on administrative needs alone, due mostly to poor communication practices between healthcare institutions and doctors, redundant and inefficient tasks, and excessive paperwork.

The numbers around costs associated with billing and insurance are even more dramatic. A study in the Journal of the American Medical Association Study found that the cost of billing and insurance represents more than 14% of all doctor revenue on average, and that figure can get as high as 25% when emergency room visits are taken into account.

Insurance claim denials at US hospitals cost another $262B in 2016. Denials can occur as a result of anything from failure to obtain proper authorisation for a procedure, or improper data entry. While hospitals recoup roughly 63% of claims that were initially denied by insurers, securing payment itself is a costly process with a lot of administrative overhead.

The Impact of Blockchain on the Insurance Industry

A cryptographically secured blockchain can maintain patient privacy while creating an industry-wide, synchronised repository of healthcare data, saving the industry billions every year. Blockchain technology can return control of medical data to patients, and let them share access to data on a case-by-case basis.

Rather than forcing insurers and providers to reconcile patient data across separate databases, a blockchain system for medical records could store a cryptographic signature for each record on a distributed ledger. The signature indexes the content of each document cryptographically and timestamps it, without actually storing any sensitive information on the blockchain.

Any time a change is made to the document, it's recorded on the shared ledger, allowing insurers and providers to audit medical information across organisations. Meanwhile, the blockchain could enable granular permissions settings to comply with regulations, while allowing data to be anonymised and shared for research.

Blockchain use case: MedRec

MedRec is a decentralised content management system for medical records from MIT. Rather than storing medical data directly on-chain, it indexes medical records on the blockchain, allowing records to be accessed by providers who have been granted permission. This is meant to help guarantee patient privacy, while creating an audit trail that makes it easy to find and verify patient information on the blockchain.

While MedRec remains an academic project in proof-of-concept stage, it presents a useful model for understanding how medical data can be secured through blockchain technology.

What's important to remember is that blockchain technology is not a silver bullet for the health insurance industry. Blockchain companies today in the insurance industry need to deal with significant regulatory and compliance hurdles to have any chance of success.

Car Insurance

Blockchain can improve the auto insurance industry by assisting drivers in getting more affordable quotes and resolve their accident claims faster. There will be less associated paperwork, and this will make underwriting easier as all data related to previous damages and repairs to any vehicle can be stored in a decentralized public ledger making estimating the 'Actual Cash Value' of any automobile an automated task.

Life Insurance

The life insurance industry has a lot of very involved paperwork, and the payout system is often subject to snafus making it difficult for beneficiaries to receive funds. Distributed ledger technology can combine the death claims and death registration processes by connecting insurance companies, funeral homes, the government, and beneficiaries. Event-based smart contracts could automate processing to benefit all of these players saving them time and money.

Travel Insurance

Travel insurance is the least involved perhaps of all these examples and could benefit from a decentralized mobile application to allow for micro-insurance on short international trips without the hassle. It would encourage more global coverage as we live in an increasingly borderless world. Bringing blockchain technology to the travel insurance industry can help protect travelers in the event of a flight delay without having to make multiple phone calls.

Property and Casualty insurance

P&C claims data is scattered across multiple locations controlled by different parties, making claims resolution a challenge. Blockchain technology enables automated real-time data collection and analysis, potentially making some types of P&C claims process up to 3x faster and 5x cheaper than at present. Automated "smart contracts" can greatly speed up claims processing and payouts, saving insurers over $200B a year. Property and casualty (P&C) insurance is big business, accounting for 48% of all US insurance premiums written in 2017, or a total of $576B.

Processing P&C claims is an error-prone procedure that requires significant manual data entry and coordination between different parties. By allowing policy holders and insurers to track and manage physical assets digitally, blockchain technology can codify business rules and automate claims processing through smart contracts, while providing a permanent audit trail.

Smart contracts using blockchain technology can turn paper contracts into programmable code that helps automate claims processing and calculates liabilities in insurance for all players involved. Smart contracts could save P&C insurers more than $200B a year in operating costs and lower their operating ratio by anywhere from 5 to 13 percentage points, according to BCG.

For auto insurance, a smart contract could be linked to sensors on a vehicle that automatically alert insurers when a crash occurs. The smart contract can then summon medical teams and towing services, launch the claims process, and inform the insured that help is on the way. As new information such as police reports and crash photos comes in, the smart contract can append them to the claim, facilitating a much faster payout process with minimal human intervention.

Blockchain use case: Insurwave

A collaboration of entities including EY, Guardtime, A.P. Møller-Maersk, Microsoft, and ACORD launched blockchain-powered marine hull insurance platform Insurwave in 2018. The platform is now in commercial use and was projected to handle risk for more than 1,000 commercial vessels and 500,000 automated transactions in its first twelve months of operation. The group plans to roll its platform out to other types of business insurance in the future, including cargo, aviation, and logistics.

The Insurwave platform provides real-time information on ship location, condition, and safety conditions for both insurers and insurees. When ships enter high-risk areas, such as war zones, the program detects this and factors it into underwriting and pricing calculations. Setting premiums for marine insurance is "notoriously complex," as the enterprise blockchain firm R3 puts it. Products like Insurwave are designed to ease that complexity by building an impossible-to-change audit trail.

Use Cases for Blockchain Applications in Insurance

Claims Opportunity

Claims make up a large percentage of operations at insurance companies. Custom smart contract code can accommodate the parameters of a policy and execute action automatically through trustless identity verification. The smart contract can act as a purse for funds that are not controlled exclusively by either the policyholder or insurance company. The funds can then be automatically directed to the correct party when a verified event (a claim) triggers the digital contract on the blockchain. Settling a claim can take days or weeks, and smart contracts can settle claims instantly without the need for paper documents, photocopying, and complex web portals.

Claims processing and management is one of the key business area for the insurance industry and the ability to promptly pay claim timely increases the reputation and trust by customers in purchasing insurance cover from such company. All claims processing undergoes three main process namely: submission of the claim by the insured, loss adjustment by the insurance company and other involved parties like the brokers and reinsurer and finally claims approval and payment.

Reinsurance

Reinsurance is when multiple insurance companies share the risk by purchasing insurance policies to offset the potential loss in case of significant incident or disaster. Blockchain could be a real asset within this space working to help automate calculations and rebalance. It can track funds available for claims and help companies assess financial risk and improve overall reinsurance strategy, saving both time and money.

Reinsurance protects insurers when large numbers of claims come in at once, such as during a natural disaster. Blockchain technology can reduce risk by facilitating information-sharing and cut costs by automating processes, ultimately saving reinsurers up to $10B.

The current reinsurance process is extremely complex and notoriously inefficient. With facultative reinsurance, each risk in a contract needs to be individually underwritten, and contracts typically take up to 3 months of wrangling between parties before they're signed. Insurers will typically engage multiple reinsurers, which means that data has to be exchanged between various parties to process claims. Different data standards between institutions often lead to different interpretations of how a contract should be implemented.

Blockchain technology has the potential to upend current reinsurance processes by streamlining the flow of information between insurers and reinsurers on a shared ledger. Using blockchain technology, detailed transactions around premiums and losses can exist on an insurer and reinsurer's computer systems at the same time, eliminating the need to reconcile books between institutions for each individual claim.

With data shared on an immutable ledger, reinsurers can be better equipped to allocate capital for claims nearly in real-time, allowing them to both process and settle claims more quickly without relying on primary insurers for data around each claim.

PricewaterhouseCoopers estimates that the blockchain can deliver reinsurance industry-wide savings of up to $10B by increasing operational efficiencies. This could trickle down and lead to lower insurance premiums for consumers - it's estimated that reinsurance accounts for 5% to 10% of existing insurance premiums.

Blockchain use case: B3i

B3i is a consortium formed in October 2016 by some of the biggest names in the insurance and reinsurance areas to explore the blockchain technology. Members include AIG, Allianz, Aegon, and Swiss Re.

In 2017, B3i launched a prototype of a smart contract management system for Property Cat XOL contracts, which is a type of reinsurance for catastrophe insurance. Each reinsurance contract on the platform is written as a smart contract with executable code on the same shared infrastructure. When an event - such as a hurricane or earthquake - occurs, the smart contract evaluates data sources from the participants and automatically calculates payouts to affected parties.

B3i's pilot program concluded in September of 2018, after testing and receiving feedback from 40 companies, and its live launch is planned for the beginning of 2019.

Executing reinsurance policies using blockchain technology can help reinsurance companies allocate capital and underwrite insurance policies more efficiently, bringing greater stability to the insurance industry. Rather than relying on primary insurers for data around losses, reinsurers can query the blockchain directly to provide coverage.

Customisation

Advanced technology can help attract customers with lower costs and more customised, easy-to-use interfaces. It is difficult to receive truly personalised or customised insurance policies at a reasonable rate. With increased transparency thanks to the public ledger, customers can onboard their data more securely and if they wish to share that data with other entities to onboard quickly for other insurance purposes. With public-private key technology, their data does not have to be linked to their identity, protecting them while still allowing them to benefit from automated policy customisation and easy-to-transfer personal profiles.

Real-time Claims and Payment Automation

Personalised payment plans and policies can now operate seamlessly for both insurance companies and policyholders using event-triggered smart contract technology. As events occur in real-time information from different systems work together to process the claims automatically and payout policyholders or have policyholders pay their premium or deductible. This makes for an improved customer experience and prevents loss for insurance companies while decreasing personnel related overhead.

Parametric Insurance

Filing claims is an incredibly involved process without a reliable or calculable outcome in certain circumstances. Parametric insurance functions to provide more exacting terms and conditions in the event of an accident. Parametric insurance decreases administrative workload in a claim settlement process as it is event-based policy, not dissimilar to how a smart contract works. The smart contract is the ideal piece of technology for an already event-triggered insurance policy, now rather than a person verifying the claim it can all be automated via smart contract. While parametric insurance is not as frequently used as other policies and insurance plans, parametric insurance could become an industry norm thanks to blockchain technology stepping in as the perfect vehicle to manage these more customised policies.

Underwriting

The underwriting process takes a highly skilled and qualified individual to determine how much coverage a policyholder will get and how much it will cost. It takes high-level data analysis to underwrite, and it is currently a very time intensive process. Using blockchain data storage management and analysis tools, underwriters can decrease risk liability and automated the policy pricing process, leading to a more cost-efficient insurance model and customer-friendly experience. It can also bring an element of transparency to the underwriting process to help build trust between customers and insurance companies that is a present pain point.

Big Data

Data management and more efficient storage might be one of the most significant use cases for insurance companies. It can improve not only data storage and security but how data is transferred and shared to streamline processes that involve multiple parties and are authentication-heavy. Blockchain can help insurance companies plan for a better future and improve how they distributed policies and settle claims daily. Using timestamp and digital fingerprinting, a more transparent, private, and secure repository for shared data is created. This helps to facilitate more affordable coverage delivered seamlessly.

Blockchain Startups Transforming the Insurance Industry:

Black – A digital insurance company on the blockchain, **opening the centralized insurance market for crowdfunding**.

B3i – A startup providing insurance solutions on a blockchain platform offering **opportunities for efficiency, growth, and quality** across the value chain.

ChainThat – Delivering business efficiency by **coordinating and streamlining operational processes** across business networks.

Inmediate – **Make policies transparent and trustworthy** by using smart contracts, powered by the Zilliqa blockchain solution.

Lemonade – A startup that offers homeowners and renters **insurance powered by artificial intelligence, blockchain, and behavioural economics**.

RiskBazaar – A peer-to-peer (P2P) **risk contacts marketplace** that lets consumers enter contracts with their friends within seconds.

Teambrella – A **P2P insurance service app** powered by blockchain.

Tierion – Turns the blockchain into a platform for **verifying any data, files, or processes**.

Blockchain in Banking

An estimated 90% of European and North American banks were exploring blockchain in 2018, according to research by Accenture. The financial sector also spent over half a billion dollars on blockchain in the same year. The global blockchain technology market is estimated to accumulate $20 billion in revenue by 2024 and the industry predicts a 30% reduction in infrastructure costs.

The financial sector has been at the forefront of blockchain adoption as it promises to drive greater transparency and veracity across the digital information ecosystem. According to a report issued by Santander: the use of blockchain could lead to cost savings in the region of up to US$20 billion yearly by 2022. The disruption that distributed ledger technology is bringing to the sector has been welcomed by some and pushed back by others. If fully adopted, it will enable entities to process payments more quickly and more accurately while reducing transaction processing costs and requirements for exceptions.

Blockchain-powered tools are intended to automate banking, creating an entire banking ecosystem based on convenience. Some examples of automation involve self-execution of financial products e.g. loans, round-the-clock deposits and transfers to enable faster transactions with, in some cases, no need for human oversight.

To achieve widespread adoption, the establishment of stable protocols and reliable networks is key. Generating internal momentum for blockchain integration and implementation and ensuring high level security are other critical aspects that need credible demonstration to encourage uptake.

Educating key stakeholders within organisations about the fundamentals of blockchain technology should be a priority and responsive organisations are already taking this important leap as reports indicate that about 73% of financial sector players currently engage outside consultants to deliver the know-how required to pull off the much needed transformation to utilise the technological advancements offered by blockchain.

Institutions and corporations continue to explore the benefits and potential competitive risks and threats this technology poses to the soundness of their financial product offerings, delivery systems and infrastructure in an effort to meet the demands of technologically savvy customers who increasingly expect traditional financial institutions to bring these innovations to market for their benefit, otherwise they'll continue to resort to service and product offers by new market entrants. Customer retention strategies within some organisations anticipate capabilities enabled by blockchain will be some of the core drivers for future success in end-user retention.

Blockchain brings enhanced accuracy and information-sharing into the financial services ecosystem and financial institutions such as Swiss bank UBS and UK-based Barclays have been on record stating that they are already experimenting with blockchain as a way to expedite back office functions and settlements. In May 2019, Barclays invested in **Crowdz**, a blockchain-based B2B payments startup that helps companies collect payments and automate digital invoices.

Cross-border payments total around $600 billion annually, and the market is set to maintain its recent growth of around 3 percent a year, driven by international trade despite considerably high fees that are sometimes up to 10% of transaction value. However, with blockchain-based transfers predicted to reduce the cost of cross-border transactions, which according to McKinsey accounted for 27% of global transaction revenue in 2017, many financial institutions have cause for concern as far as losing market share if they don't consider a blockchain strategy. McKinsey also estimates that blockchains applied to cross-border payments could save about $4 billion a year.

Already projects like **Ripple** have partnered with financial institutions such as Santander and Western Union with the goal of improving the efficiency of cross-border transactions. Big corporations like JP Morgan have also entered the blockchain space with the announcement of the JPM Coin, which it intends to use to facilitate transactions between institutional accounts. In 2017, Australia and New Zealand Banking Group, JPMorgan Chase, and Royal Bank of Canada launched the Interbank Information Network (IIN), a cross-border payments service. "By leveraging blockchain technology, IIN will significantly reduce the number of participants currently needed to respond to compliance and other data-related inquiries that delay payments," JPMorgan Chase said in a statement.

Some blockchain providers are already active in payments. Ripple connects banks and payments providers via RippleNet, allowing them to make payments with fiat currency or Ripple's own XRP cryptocurrency. The network is based on a private, non-distributed ledger, which relies on a limited ecosystem of correspondent banks. Fintech in general is increasing competition and leading to more efficiency in the value chain and numerous incumbents are developing their own solutions. The Society for Worldwide Interbank Financial Telecommunications (SWIFT), for example, is working with banks through its global payments innovation initiative to improve the cross-border payments experience.

Africa and developing economies will be impact most by blockchain. Blockchain startup **BanQu** is already working with AB InBev to facilitate payments to cassava farmers in Zambia. BanQu's platform tracks the farmers' products through the supply chain and then provides digital payments to farmers via their mobile phones, even if they don't have bank accounts. Virgin Money recently **announced** a new digital service offering in South Africa which will include a blockchain-based digital wallet.

Blockchain, Financial Markets &

Trading Systems

Technology makes it possible for stock markets to be more efficient. Today, stock trades are often executed in milliseconds by algorithms. With artificial intelligence powering these algorithms, large volumes of market data, brokerage reports, company annual reports and results are able to be processed to make 'smart' decisions in high frequency trades.

Settling trades involves co-ordinating payment and delivery and then reconciling records. In huge financial centres, trades sometimes take a couple of days to settle, which is one reason why several stock exchanges are looking into whether distributed ledgers could speed up these processes. The traditional model used for settling trades and ensuring proper share ownership is now seen as inefficient and blockchain technology proponents are advocating for decentralised securities platforms which would enable the settlement of trades to occur through a blockchain. Essentially, the argument is that the technology can be used in stock trading to speed up settlements.

Blockchain is also deemed as a potential solution to fundraising and asset management, margin financing, post-trade settling, tracking securities lending, and systemic risk monitoring. Furthermore, blockchain technology could also help reduce costs levied on customers by eliminating the need for middlemen when it comes to executing some of the necessary functions in facilitating stock market trades.

Asset classes that can be adopted for blockchain

Cash equity

The settlement of cash equity can be reduced to T+0 from the current T+3 settlement cycle. There will be automatic reconciliation, as all the participants/nodes will be sharing the same ledger. Similarly, the front and back offices will be relying on the same ledger, leading to increased operational efficiency.

Fixed income

These trades are based on fixed contract parameters, and could be the ideal asset class for blockchain validation. However, fixed income securities are currently settled on a T+0 basis, and thus, adopting blockchain will not add much value in reducing the settlement cycle.

IRS, Equity Options, Futures, and Repos

Blockchain can simplify processing of the trade lifecycle, maintain one common ledger among the participants, and use smart contracts to trigger period payment(s) based on events. As the blocks made are immutable and maintain all the records from the start, an efficient audit trail can be maintained.

Exotic derivatives

Standardised terms and conditions will allow automatic validation of economic parameters and adding to a blockchain, with automatic payoff triggered by events and automated settlements. A distributed ledger will also allow transparency to other participants of verified asset holdings.

Blockchain in Over-the-Counter Derivatives

The use of distributed ledger systems and smart contracts is likely to enhance efficiencies in transacting derivative products in the OTC market.

The benefits of using blockchain technology can include:
- Automating the execution of OTC agreements by using smart contracts on the blockchain network, wherein agreement terms can be implemented and confirmed without any human intervention.

- Peer-to-peer architecture will allow parties in an OTC trade to transact directly with their counterpart, without the need of a third-party.
- Maintaining the same ledger with both sides of the transaction increases transparency, which allows counterparties to view the data during the life cycle of the swap.
- Regulators can access any information in real time, by using their authorised nodes in the blockchain network.

A few notable initiatives in this area include that of Axoni, a technology firm that specialises in distributed ledger infrastructure, along with eleven other firms such as BNP Paribas, Citi, Credit Suisse, Canada Pension Plan Investment Board, Goldman Sachs, and JP Morgan. They announced the completion of a pilot test to manage equity swap transactions and related post-trade lifecycle events. In June 2017, a group of Japanese banks, including Nomura and Mizuho Financial, started testing OTC derivative contracts on a blockchain platform developed by R3.

Trade Processing Using Blockchain

Reconciliation

The main benefit expected from using blockchain technology in the capital market is the reduction of intermediaries involved in processing of trades, thereby reducing costs and effort that goes in reconciling information.

Trade Validation

Blockchain supports smart contracts, where rules of the contract are embedded into a code or deployed on the blockchain. The introduction of the smart contract technology could validate contractual data by entering the distributed ledger, which should make processing simpler and reduce exception correction time. The nodes in the network can monitor and detect contracts for changes of ownership and contract rules. This would enhance trade validation in terms of efficiency. The trade validation on blockchain is applicable mainly for contract-based asset trades, basic cash equities and fixed income, repurchase agreements, and swap transactions across all asset classes. As any record written to the distributed ledger is immutable, any modifications, cancellations and corrections can only be done by "reverse" transactions.

Reference Data

Reference data consists of asset or security information, calendar days, ticker symbols, client data, and so on, and is essential for processing a trade to its final settlement. Companies across the industry store reference data in their own legacy systems, resulting in highly time-consuming reconciliations with data of other participants involved in the trade.

In addition, data reconciliation is necessary between internal systems within an enterprise. The common reference data can be implemented on blockchain, with its standardised validation rules among the participants in the network and auditable change history. This would allow regulators and other participants to view how the data record is being created in the ledger in real time, and which nodes validate the data creation.

Netting and Clearing

In blockchain, the question is whether it will settle trades either on a gross or net basis. Some advocate that blockchain can allow delay in trades, so these can be netted at the blockchain level, thereby reducing risk and liquidity requirements. Further, clearing to reduce settlement failure (in addition to multilateral netting) using central counterparty for each trade could also be deployed in blockchain, through appropriate rules.

Faster Settlement

In theory, the blockchain technology could reduce processes involved in clearing and settlement, because once a transaction is confirmed and committed to the ledger, the associated token (digital representation of an asset or any sensitive data element) is simultaneously settled in the digital wallet of the beneficial owner. The faster settlement is likely to reduce costs, and lower settlement risks.

Collateral Management

This can be embedded into blockchain in the form of smart contracts, which will contain rules to automate triggering of margin calls, and so on. As both the sender and receiver are on the same blockchain network, the movement of digital recording of assets through tokens substitute sensitive data with a non-sensitive equivalent with the ability to track asset movement, and proper design and rules allow exchange of assets for collateral purposes. This can also be extended to the distributed ledger technology.

Regulatory Reporting

As all the participants will be maintaining one version of the truth, there will be no need for costly reconciliation. Regulators will have visibility of transaction in real time and have monitoring efficiency on the activities of transacting parties. Further, the current use of disparate systems, both externally and internally, provides many bottlenecks when doing Know Your Customer (KYC) and Anti Money Laundering (AML) checks.

Verification of information and repetitive information exchange between parties during client onboarding is time consuming. This is likely to be remedied when there's one version of the truth maintained among all the participants in the blockchain network.

Audit Trail

As all entries are written on the ledger, falsification of such records in order to conceal activity is practically impossible. In addition, as companies can write their transactions directly into a distributed ledger, it eliminates the requirement to keep separate records based on transaction receipts. Given the digitised nature of transactions, auditing of such transactions can also be done electronically, eliminating much of the manual work, and the time and cost associated with it. Another important aspect of blockchain is that each block has a reference to its previous block, thereby maintaining a full history of all transactions and providing a completely traceable audit trail.

Adoption of blockchain for stock exchanges

Stock exchanges can run using a blockchain, with no need for a centralised settlement or transfer of share certificates. This is cheaper, faster, reduces risks, and more secure. Blockchain allows different banks to do business with each other more easily and across borders. By shifting reliance away from central banks, the conduct of business is more flexible and manageable.

Santander was the first UK bank to use blockchain technology to transfer live international payments. Payments of between £10 and £10,000 can be made, around the clock. American Express and Santander have partnered with Ripple for cross-border payments via blockchain. The partnership is said to have enabled the speeding up of cross-border payments between the US and the UK.

Nasdaq has been at the forefront of the blockchain revolution. At the turn of 2015, it unveiled the use of its Nasdaq Linq Blockchain Ledger technology. Nasdaq and Citi announced an integrated payment solution using a distributed ledger to record and transmit payment instructions based on **Chain**'s blockchain technology.

Australian Stock Exchange (ASX) began to evaluate replacement options for the Clearing House Electronic Subregister System (CHESS) in 2015. Eventually, ASX selected U.S.-based blockchain startup Digital Asset Holdings, LLC to develop distributed ledger based solutions for clearing and settling trades.

Japan's Financial Services Agency allowed the **Japan Exchange Group(JPX)**, which operates the Tokyo Stock Exchange, to use blockchain as its core trading infrastructure. In 2015, Nasdaq unveiled the use of its Nasdaq Linq blockchain ledger technology to successfully complete and record private securities transactions. **Japan Exchange Group** and IBM are working towards testing the potential of blockchain technology for use in trading in low transaction markets.

Korea Exchange launched Korea Startup Market (KSM) with Blocko's blockchain technology to enable equity shares of startup companies to be traded in the open market.

Deutsche Börse Group has invested in the development of blockchain services including a solution for cross-border securities transfer in cooperation with the Liquidity Alliance. India's **National Stock Exchange** (NSE) conducted a blockchain trial involving the country's leading banks including IDFC, Kotak Mahindra, ICICI, IndusInd and RBL.

Moscow Exchange (MOEX) successfully conducted e-voting for bondholders via blockchain at the National Settlement Depository (**NSD**).

The **London Stock Exchange**, part of the PDTL group, is involved in improving the post-trade space using the blockchain technology.

The **Luxembourg Stock Exchange** launched a blockchain-enabled security system, where the officially generated

Signature by Appointed Mechanism (OAM), along with document type and document URL are stored in the blockchain ledger.

Santiago Exchange is also exploring blockchain for application across Chile's financial sector.

The Toronto-based **TMX Group**, operator of the Toronto Stock Exchange, announced the development of a blockchain based prototype to 'power' a new service offering from Natural Gas Exchange (NGX).

Blockchain could be the answer to interoperability, trust, and transparency issues in fragmented stock market systems. Blockchain can make stock exchanges much more optimal through automation and decentralisation. It can help reduce costs levied on customers in terms of commission while speeding up the process, resulting in fast transaction settlements. The technology can have a viable use in clearing and settlement, while securely automating the post-trade process, easing paperwork of trade and legal ownership transfer of the security. Ultimately, faster and efficient trade cycles will lead to better liquidity mechanisms and possibly more trades and investments.

The Rise of Decentralised Media

New tech is changing the media and entertainment industry. New business models are being generated to cater to consumers who are increasingly expecting media and entertainment providers to deliver better choice, convenience and value packaged in personalised and customisable experiences made available on demand and on a cross-platform basis but with little to no advertising backed by strong data protection frameworks.
Media and entertainment companies therefore need to adapt to new realities.

With intensifying competition for viewers and advertisers, combined with ongoing declines in subscribers, there is mounting pressure on topline performance at many companies across the industry. The proliferation of video distribution platforms and uplift in engagement metrics, subscription fees, advertising revenue as a consequence has created enormous competition with respect to developing and acquiring the best content. And with increasing costs of procuring content and talent new operational practices and mechanisms will inevitably be introduced.

Where does blockchain fit in?

In considering how blockchain impacts media and entertainment businesses, there are apparent risks and opportunities. For content creators, blockchain provides more control, flexible content licensing models, better content revenues and faster monetisation. For aggregators such as music businesses, publishing companies, performing rights organisations, it means less need for intermediaries and more efficient distribution of revenue across the chain which potentially makes them less relevant. However, incorporating blockchain-driven technology into existing offerings could help aggregators concentrate on activities where they can add real value. Managing contracts, relationships with labels, legacy catalogs, and even the collection of royalty payments for musical events may still require human involvement.

For distributors, the threat of disruption is much more significant. Online distributors such as Spotify and Amazon, which have reaped huge profits from the digitisation of content, may face some of the biggest risks. As content consumers are able to connect directly with content creators, distributors may play less significant roles. Even if this change takes many years to materialise, the threat is real. Like aggregators, distributors need to figure out what they provide that's distinctive beyond being an access and payment channel. To prepare for the future, they need to experiment with blockchain-enabled business models so that they can position themselves in a new digital content market built on this technology.

The state of blockchain-based technologies in media and entertainment – what progress has been made?

Monetising value continues to present significant challenges despite new business models emerging in the media and entertainment industries. Newspapers and magazines still struggle to monetise value due to the unlimited free content and limited mechanisms for protecting intellectual property.

Advertising revenue has shifted to social media and search platforms. In the music world, for example, digital content distribution via streaming is beneficial to major record labels and top-tier artists. But it isn't commercially viable for smaller labels or average musicians, who receive only a tiny fraction of the revenue generated from their music.

Companies have started building innovative business models that not only offer new monetisation strategies for their digital assets but also streamline critical business activities such as relationships with business partners and distribution of revenue across the value chain. These developments could create completely new ecosystems for content creation and consumption.

Monetising content for creators and curators

The first new business model involves creating a social network in which users can earn financial rewards (in the form of micropayments or payments of digital currency) by posting their own content or curating and promoting others' posts. Rather than allowing the platform owners to reap all the monetary benefits, as happens today with established players like Facebook and LinkedIn, this model compensates independent content creators (bloggers, experts, hobbyists) and consumers (social network users who enjoy sharing their opinions) for their contributions.

For example, Steemit, a blockchain-based social network, rewards content creators with digital currency (called "Steem") based on the popularity of their posts. Although it was initially geared toward users interested in the topic of cryptocurrency, the content focus has expanded to include technology, science, news, art, food, photography, and travel. As a post is upvoted and becomes popular, the author's reward increases, and early promoters can earn a slice of that. The platform also generates reputation scores for users. According to the Steemit website, this system helps foster the creation and curation of quality content.

Steemit isn't alone in rewarding users financially. **Yours**, also pays content creators and allows them to set their own rates for how much they will receive when someone reads or views a post. Authors and artists can even charge users for the right to comment. Compensating users on both sides represents an entirely new concept for monetizing social network activity.

Whereas Facebook's and LinkedIn's business models rely on targeted advertising based on insights drawn from a user's platform activity history, blockchain-based social media platforms aim to monetize the relationships between authors and their followers, thus stimulating the creation of new content. Letting users monetize their own content is a key element in attracting users to the social networks. However, there are different mechanisms for monetization available to platform owners as well. Yours uses a commission model and charges fees for transactions that occur on its platform. For now, Steemit is using an approach that's closely linked to the value of its own cryptocurrency, although its revenue model is still evolving.

Creating a one-stop content shop

The second new business model simplifies the value chain by decreasing or eliminating the need for intermediaries between users who create content and those who consume it. The model does away with many of the traditional steps and layers, such as content aggregation and distribution, thereby reducing the amount of time it takes to bring new content to consumers and realize revenue. It relies heavily on cryptocurrency and blockchain-based applications like smart contracts and smart property to facilitate and process direct transactions between creators and consumers.

One company that uses this model is **Breaker**, formerly, SingularDTV, a blockchain film and television studio and distribution portal. **Breaker** caters to video and film producers by giving artists more control over their work, allowing them to launch, distribute, and monetise content without the usual intervention from studios or production houses and without being tied to exclusivity agreements with distribution channels. At the same time, it uses smart contracts to enable consumers to browse, access, and pay for content instantaneously with digital currency.

Similarly, startups **Creativechain** and **Musicoin** offer their own marketplaces for digital content, where creators and consumers can interact without intermediaries. Creativechain targets artists, including musicians, designers, and writers, using a blockchain designed to support content registration, distribution, and monetisation. Artists can choose from different licensing methods, ranging from free distribution to paid limited editions.

This flexibility lets them select the method that is best suited to distributing their work. Under this scenario, there is no need for third-party distributors to bring the content to consumers and collect revenue; the platform handles that directly. Musicoin, meanwhile, focuses exclusively on the music industry and encourages independent artists to register and publish their work on its own blockchain-based platform. It uses a standard pay-per-play smart contract to reward musicians based on preset fees each time a song gets played. In addition, consumers are encouraged to reward their favourite artists with tips. Besides distributors, other players typically involved in music rights management (including what are known as "performing rights organisations," which essentially collect royalties for music performance on behalf of rights owners) are not needed on this platform since it connects music consumers directly to artists or labels and automatically customises revenue distribution.

The startups adopting this business model are capturing revenue in different ways. Since content is being sold and payment transactions are handled in the platform, one straightforward monetisation strategy is to charge commission fees. Other options companies are considering are licensing platforms for use by third parties and creating and selling original content. In addition, some startups are following an open-source model: The platform is published as free software, and the startup works to drive its further development while earning money by providing services like consulting, training, or onboarding. As with the previous business model (monetising content for both creators and curators), one-stop content shops are still experimenting with different revenue model options until the most effective ones consolidate.

Monetising content and building a one-stop content shop were the most disruptive. In both instances, companies are starting small by serving a low-end market niche (for example, indie music labels and their audiences) with a value proposition aligned with users' goals (helping both artists and consumers capture more financial value and making their transactions less cumbersome). Because the underlying blockchain technology is not sufficiently mature to handle billions of users and millions of content titles, startups are not yet able to challenge established mass-market players like Facebook, Amazon Prime, and Netflix. But that's partly what makes the new models serious threats: Industry leaders might not recognise them as threats in time to protect themselves.

As the technology matures and the blockchain-enabled startups begin serving broader segments of customers with a wider range of content, for instance, or ad-free social media environments, it will be the beginning of a new era in the media and entertainment industry.

Blockchain, IoT, & Critical

Infrastructure Security

Cyber-security is a top concern for many organisations, especially those handling and processing sensitive data. Data remains a primary target for attackers. Microsoft predicts that by 2020, data volumes will be 50 times what they are today. It is estimated that approximately 111 billion new software codes are produced every year which translates to billions of vulnerabilities that attackers can exploit.

Gartner's research revealed that worldwide information security is expected to hit US$93 billion in 2018. According to Cisco's 2017 annual report on cyber-security, 20% of the organisations surveyed had had significant data breaches within a 12-month period. This backs research carried out by entities such as Cybersecurity Ventures which predict that global cybersecurity spending will exceed $1 trillion cumulatively over a period of five years and that cybercrime damages will rise in cost from $3 trillion in 2015 to $6 trillion in 2021.

Ed Powers, a Cyber Risk Lead at Deloitte's U.S. has been on record stating that "while still nascent, there is promising innovation in blockchain towards helping enterprises tackle immutable Cyber Risk challenges such as digital identities and maintaining data integrity."

Blockchain-powered Cybersecurity

Blockchains could potentially help improve cyber defence by securing and preventing fraudulent activities through consensus mechanisms, and detecting data tampering based on the key strengths of the technology which include immutability, transparency, auditability, data encryption & operational resilience due to distributed network systems having no single point of failure. Consensus-based control distributes the responsibility of security across nodes within a blockchain network, making it impossible for hackers to infiltrate such a network. Decentralisation makes cybersecurity solutions highly scalable by addressing one of the biggest concerns of implementing cybersecurity on an expanding network such as in the case of connected devices.

Blockchain technology alongside IoT promises to improve the security of connected devices by cryptographically securing and storing communication among IoT devices in tamper-proof logs. A blockchain-based cybersecurity platform can secure connected devices using digital signatures to identify and authenticate them, adding them as authorized participants in the blockchain network and ring-fencing critical infrastructure by rendering them invisible to unauthorized access attempts.

Enterprise Protection: Beating the Bug

A cybersecurity solution based on blockchain technology offers a future-proof way to secure IoT devices, networks and communications. Blockchain is already showing great promise in the energy supply chain security and management. Studies, validations and verifications of blockchain applications to tackle cyber security challenges are already underway and some companies are seriously making efforts to learn how technologies such as blockchain could help secure and optimise their complex systems.

Companies like **Xage** are employing blockchain's tamperproof ledgers to share security data across industrial device networks. Using its blockchain-enabled KSI (Keyless Signature Infrastructure), cybersecurity startup **Guardtime** tags and verifies data transactions. These are just a few of the many use cases under development which are blockchain-based.

As critical infrastructure like power plants and transportation become equipped with connected sensors, attack risks go higher and the need for better security becomes even more critical. If blockchain technology gains wider adoption, critical infrastructure will be better protected. With over 45 billion IoT devices expected to be connected by 2021, according to a report by Juniper Research and the cumulative cost of data breaches between 2017 and 2022 expected to reach $8 trillion, it is imperative that critical infrastructure projects begin to research and develop solutions that will ensure that key security systems are not compromised.

Commercial Real Estate in a

Digital Asset Economy

Historically, the real estate industry has lagged in adopting new technology. However, research shows that implementation of blockchain technology can have a range of benefits for the sector going into the future. According to **Deloitte**blockchain technology has recently been adopted and adapted for use by the commercial real estate (CRE) industry.

CRE executives are finding that blockchain-based smart contracts can play a much larger role in their industry. Real estate interactions are third-party dependent making them costly and time-consuming. From rentals to larger commercial deals, smart contract technology can be deployed to make for real estate transactions safer and easier. Blockchain can potentially transform core commercial real estate operations such as property transactions like purchase, sale, financing, leasing, and management transactions.

Blockchain technology can also assist in the creation of new business models connecting potential buyers and sellers. Asset tokenisation on blockchain has opened up another huge market because it enables property to be traded similar to other exchange-based securities. It also presents the opportunity to sell into new market segments as a result of lower costs. The opening of new geographical markets as a result of secure identities and widening of investment opportunities through new options for asset-funding is also made possible by blockchain.

Through asset tokenisation opportunities for new investment products and new revenue sources created by direct connection to end investors, bypassing the wholesale market and distribution platforms are available. Furthermore, blockchain enables enhanced data management capabilities, ore efficient post-trade processes, more efficient reporting and oversight, reduced counter-party risk and enhanced collateral management on top of reduced costs.

Use Cases for Blockchain Applications in Real Estate

Property Search

Blockchain can allow a property listing to exist on a single decentralized database and market participants could access more reliable data at a lower cost. With data distributed across a peer-to-peer network, brokers would be able to have more control over their data, as it would be more difficult for it to be interfered with by any third parties. **Imbrex** is an example of such a blockchain-based property listing platform.

Property Management

Property management is highly complex, with many stakeholders involved — including landlords, property managers, tenants, and vendors. Most properties are currently managed either offline through manual paperwork, or through multiple software programs that generally don't integrate well with one another. Through the use of a single decentralised application that uses blockchain-backed smart contracts, the entire property management process, from signing lease agreements to managing cash flow to filing maintenance requests, can be conducted in a secure and transparent manner.

In residential real estate, for example, a landlord and tenant could digitally sign a smart contract agreement that includes information such as rental value, payment frequency, and details of both the tenant and property. Based on the agreed upon terms, the smart contract could automatically initiate lease payments from the tenant to the landlord, as well as to any contractors that perform periodic maintenance. Upon termination of the lease, the smart contract could also be set to automatically send payment of the security deposit back to the tenant.

Titles

Blockchain could make title investigations much easier for those in the real estate business. The result will be faster closings and lowered risk for error during title transfers. Blockchain can provide better property ownership record tracking, and improve efficiencies for title companies and title insurance. Most property titles are paper-based, creating opportunities for errors and fraud. According to the American Land Title Association, title professionals find defects in 25% of all titles during the transaction process. This means that property owners often incur high legal fees to ensure authenticity and accuracy of their property titles.

Title fraud also presents a risk to homeowners. In the US, losses associated with title fraud reportedly averaged roughly $103,000 per case in 2015, which contributed to large numbers of property buyers purchasing title insurance. These title management issues could potentially be mitigated by using blockchain technology to build immutable digital records of land titles. This approach could simplify property title management, making it more transparent and helping to reduce the risk of title fraud and the need for additional insurance.

Some companies and governments are looking to implement blockchain technology for the title management process. In 2017, the company partnered with the Brazilian *Cartorio de Registro de Imoveis* (Real Estate Registry) to establish pilot programs. Ghanaian blockchain company Bitland has been working on a similar solution for Ghana, where it is estimated that almost 80% of land is unregistered, according to Forbes. Those that possess unregistered land find it more difficult to prove legal ownership, increasing their exposure to the risk of land seizures or property theft.

Bitland is seeking to create secure digital public records of ownership on its blockchain platform, with the aim of protecting land owners from title fraud. Bitland has expanded to operate in 7 African nations, India, and is also working with Native Americans in the US.

Real estate giant RE/MAX has also been exploring blockchain use cases. RE/MAX partnered with blockchain company **XYO Network** to explore using blockchain technology to build a decentralized online land title registry in Mexico. XYO Network's first project with RE/MAX involves tying location coordinates to unique digital tokens that represent land titles. As a property changes owners so will the digital token (with the transaction being recorded on a blockchain), establishing a transparent history of land ownership.

SafeChain is another enterprise leveraging blockchain technology in the title management space. The company helps title agents verify client identities, bank account ownership, and securely transfer wire information. Its platform seeks to reduce losses from fraud and bring down operational costs.

Real Estate Investing

Real estate investing has historically only been available to those able to put down large sums of capital. In addition, real estate investing often involves expensive intermediaries such as fund managers, further raising the barrier to entry.

However, blockchain technology it looking to disrupt real estate investing by providing a way to decentralise the process through crowdsourcing and tokenisation. This approach makes it easier to establish a market for property "micro-shares," creating the potential for a property to effectively have numerous co-owners with a stake in potential returns.

There are many blockchain-based real estate investment platforms that currently exist, though most are still in the development phase. One that is more established is **BitofProperty**. The Singapore-based company has built a blockchain-based crowdfunding platform that allows users to invest in both residential and commercial rental properties. Users receive monthly income from the properties they have invested in.

Another example is **Brickblock**, a smart contract platform which is seeking to use tokenized real estate to help developers raise capital for projects. Brickblock has received almost $6M in funding from Finch Capital and has several partnerships, including with JTC Group, solarisBank, and Peakside Capital.

Real Estate Investment Trusts (REIT)

Blockchain applications and REIT are a match made in heaven. From shareholder communication to dividend distribution, REIT can benefit end-to-end from decentralization. Smart contracts can execute upon event according to predetermined conditions. REITs can crowdfund using digital IPOs. Investors can receive funds in a timelier fashion not having to wait for REITs to make good on paper contracts.

Smart Contract Escrow

This might be the most viable use case for blockchain applications in real estate. Smart contracts double as escrow and create a safe repository for funds to then be trustless-ly released to the verified parties when triggered by event confirmation. Rather than tenants sending landlords checks every month in the mail, tenants can have a multi-signature transaction with the use of public-private key cryptography. Security deposits can be held in escrow for the duration of the lease and only returned at the end upon two out of three parties (third being an arbitrator) using their private key.

Blockchain Notarisation

Real estate paperwork authentication often requires a notary. Buyer and seller sign an agreement and then the transaction can be recorded on the smart contract, and this agreement then receives designated a hash. The buyer then can obtain the address of the smart contract to send the funds to the correct blockchain-based locale.

Notarisation can now happen on-chain as the seller goes to the notary with the smart contract address and sign the final document without the presence of the buyer. The notary is then able to use their private key to mark the deal executed on the blockchain. In the future, as governments accept blockchain transactions as trustless, the notary can be eliminated from the process.

Ownership Verification

Property history databases are never up-to-date and are certainly not transparent in their origins or motives. Using blockchain to track the history of repairs and issues a property experiences can later help sellers improve resale value or make buyers aware of the property's troubled past. A home inspection would also be either unnecessary or a less involved task. Home inspectors could contribute to databases to make sure property issues are part of the immutable records. This would help buyers feel more confident in their purchases knowing the full history of the property.

Financing and Payment Systems and Lending Process

Depending on a bank to approve a loan and set interest rates for mortgages can be lengthy and expensive, sometimes impossible process. P2P lending facilitated by on-chain technology can break down the barriers for home ownership for those with bad credit or past debt who otherwise should be eligible for a loan. Borrowing from a network of lenders rather than just one results in lower interest rates and service fees, above all else, it creates an opening for those who would otherwise be ineligible or face incredible interest rates.

Due to the extensive documentation required and the involvement of various intermediaries, existing modes of financing and payments for property transactions are currently slow, expensive, and opaque. These issues are especially pronounced when a property is financed through a mortgage and when international transactions are required.

The current process for mortgage approval for residential properties takes on average around 30-60 days to complete, according to the National Association of Realtors. For commercial real estate - which is more complex to process than residential real estate - the time it takes to get approved can be even longer, often requiring around 90 days.

This process could be simplified and made more transparent when blockchain technology is applied. For example, verifiable digital identities for properties could allow a reduction in both due diligence and loan documentation time, thus speeding up the mortgage approval process.
The borrower and lender could also use blockchain technology to execute an immutable smart contract-based loan document, fully accessible by all legal parties involved. Adoption of blockchain technology could save the US mortgage loan industry up to 20% in expenses per year, according to a report published by Moody's Investor Service, which would amount to $1.7B in annual savings.

ShelterZoom is a startup aiming to streamline real estate transactions by putting all the processes on the Ethereum blockchain.

Real estate agents, buyers, sellers, and renters can view offers and acceptances on the platform, which also allows access to property titles, mortgages, legal documents, and home inspection reports.

ShelterZoom has partnered with over 90 brokerages around the world, including RE/MAX Revolution in Boston, Massachusetts.

Ripple connects banks and payment providers on RippleNet, its private blockchain, seeking to provide a payment platform for transferring money globally. One use case for Ripple is facilitating cross-border real estate payments. All parties involved in a real estate transaction can be connected on an online platform, view past transactions between parties, and make payments. The company claims that its approach allows transactions to be secure, quick, and low cost - a compelling proposition compared to the high fees and multi-day wait associated with traditional international payment systems.

Tenant Screening and Leasing Process

Manual pen and paper tenant screening is still common practice in the real estate industry. Landlords do not have a centralised hub to verify tenants through immutable data stores detailing rental history. Landlords have to conduct background checks with only the information provided to them by the tenant. Renter fraud is a common woe for property owners who have no tried and true way to screen tenants.

Instead, they are forced to conduct credit and rental history checks themselves. If landlords and tenants could use blockchain to complete all rental-associated tasks on a p2p network, this could help standardise pre-authenticated on-chain renter and landlord profiles with immutable histories and reputation scores to help tenants avoid slum lords, and landlords prevent rent dodgers. P2P rental networks could also help renters crowdsource deposits to reduce the need to hold their own funds in a smart contract for a year or more.

Due Diligence and Financial Evaluation Process

Physical paper documents for proof of identity are still the norm today. This approach requires the commitment of significant time and effort for due diligence and financial verification. This manual verification process also increases the likelihood of errors and can involve multiple third-party service providers. These factors can be costly and slow down the due diligence process.

Using digital identities on the blockchain, this entire process can be taken online in a secure manner - increasing efficiency, lowering costs, enhancing data security, and reducing the chance of manual errors.

For example, a real estate property's digital identity could consolidate information such as vacancy, tenant profile, financial and legal status, and performance metrics. A digital blockchain-based solution is currently being developed by Lantmäteriet, the Swedish land authority, in collaboration with blockchain startup **ChromaWay**, Swedish telecommunications giant Telia Company, and several real estate enterprises.

Its goal is to digitise contracts for sale and property mortgages that are authenticated by blockchain technology. This solution streamlines the process of transferring property titles while also adding some layers of security. All parties involved in the process, including the buyer, seller, real estate agent, the buyer's bank, and the land registry, have their own digital identities.

Each can use a single application to securely send and sign official documents using blockchain-verified smart contracts. All actors can view the associated documents and information, with verification of the steps that have taken place during the process.

ChromaWay announced that it had completed a full transaction on the platform in June 2018. Other organisations around the world are also making blockchain real estate strides. Bank of China Hong Kong (BOCHK), for example, stated in mid-2018 that it processes 85% of real estate appraisals using its own private blockchain.

BOCHK's General Manager of Information Technology Rocky Cheng Chung-ngam said, "In the past, banks and [real estate] appraisers had to exchange faxes and emails to produce and deliver physical certificates. Now the process can be done on blockchain in seconds."

Managing Commissions

Smart contracts aren't just used for buyer-seller or renter-landlord interactions. They can also be used to help real estate companies better manage their resources and fund distribution. It is common for multiple agents to be working on a single listing creating commission distribution hiccups. For multi-broker listings, everyone gets paid a percentage of the commission as described in paper commission-splitting agreements. Smart contracts can easily automate this process and companies can avoid the associated overhead that is involved in figuring out who gets what, how and when. Brokers and agents benefit from automated commission splitting as they will no longer have to wait for their funds, they can receive payment the same day the deal is closed.

Sources:

https://assets.kpmg/content/dam/kpmg/ng/pdf/advisory/ng-leading-through-digital.pdf

https://www.lntinfotech.com/wp-content/uploads/2018/05/How-Blockchain-is-Transforming-Capital-Market.pdf

https://www.cbinsights.com/research/blockchain-insurance-disruption/

https://www.blockchaintechnologies.com/applications/

https://www.who.int/news-room/detail/28-11-2017-1-in-10-medical-products-in-developing-countries-is-substandard-or-falsified

https://sloanreview.mit.edu/article/blockchain-is-changing-how-media-and-entertainment-companies-compete/

https://www.ey.com/en_us/tmt/ten-opportunities-and-threats-for-media-and-entertainment-compan

https://hbr.org/2017/01/the-truth-about-blockchain

https://thefintechworld.com/blockchain/f/how-blockchain-is-impacting-real-estate?blogcategory=Blockchain

https://www.investopedia.com/terms/b/blockchain.asp

https://www2.deloitte.com/content/dam/Deloitte/us/Documents/financial-services/us-dcfs-blockchain-in-cre-the-future-is-here.pdf

www.ingramcontent.com/pod-product-compliance
Lightning Source LLC
Chambersburg PA
CBHW031246050326
40690CB00007B/977